For my wife, Susan, and son, Josh,
who love Christmas music all year long.

STAR of WONDER, STAR of NIGHT

SEASONAL PIANO ARRANGEMENTS

by Philip Kern

CONTENTS

GlorySound

A DIVISION OF SHAWNEE PRESS, INC.
EXCLUSIVELY DISTRIBUTED BY HAL LEONARD CORPORATION

Visit Shawnee Press Online at
www.shawneepress.com

FOREWORD

One might wonder if the world needs another collection of piano arrangements for Christmas. There are dozens out there, many of them quite good. But as an arranger, I find the melodies contained in this collection to be so deeply ingrained in the message of Christmas that they are boundless in possibilities. Ten different arrangements of "Silent Night, Holy Night" will give you ten different ways of hearing the same perennial favorite, each with something unique to say.

These piano arrangements are suitable for liturgical and recital/concert settings. The intermediate pianist will find them both satisfying and challenging. You will explore asymmetric meter (7/8 time signature in "He is Born, the Divine Christ Child"), jazz piano technique ("Go, Tell It on the Mountain"), variation technique ("Ding! Dong! Merrily on High") and a host of contemporary performance practices for the piano.

My thanks go to Joseph M. Martin, Director of Church Publications at Shawnee Press, for selecting this collection to be published. Lee Dengler has also brought a gracious and diligent professionalism to the editing of these pages.

To create fresh, contemporary arrangements of beloved Christmas melodies has been my goal. May each piece be a blessing to the holidays.

Philip Kern
May, 2011

COME, THOU LONG-EXPECTED JESUS

Arranged by
PHILIP KERN (ASCAP)

Tune: **HYFRYDOL**
by ROWLAND H. PRICHARD (1811-1887)

GO, TELL IT ON THE MOUNTAIN

Arranged by
PHILIP KERN (ASCAP)

Tune: **GO TELL IT**
Traditional Spiritual

With a driving swing feel (♩ = ca. 76)

IT CAME UPON THE MIDNIGHT CLEAR

Arranged by
PHILIP KERN (ASCAP)

Tune: **CAROL**
by RICHARD STORRS WILLIS (1819-1900)

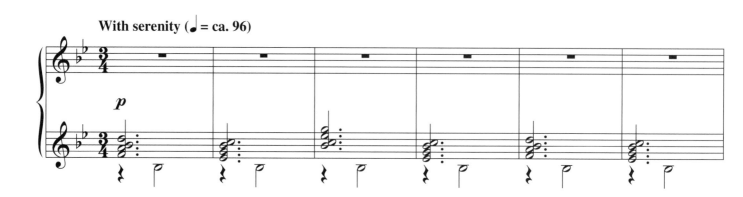

Copyright © 2011 by HAL LEONARD CORPORATION
International Copyright Secured. All Rights Reserved.

COPYING IS ILLEGAL

DING! DONG! MERRILY ON HIGH
Variations

Arranged by
PHILIP KERN (ASCAP)

Traditional French Carol
from *Orchésographie*
THOINOT ARBEAU, 1588

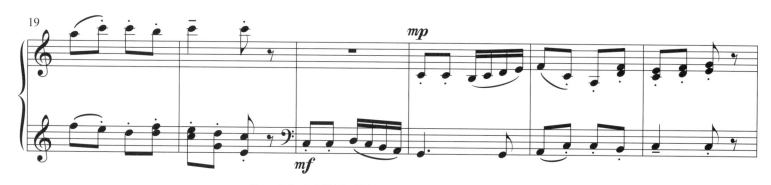

INFANT HOLY, INFANT LOWLY

Arranged by
PHILIP KERN (ASCAP)

Tune: **W ZLOBIE LEZY**
by Traditional Polish Carol

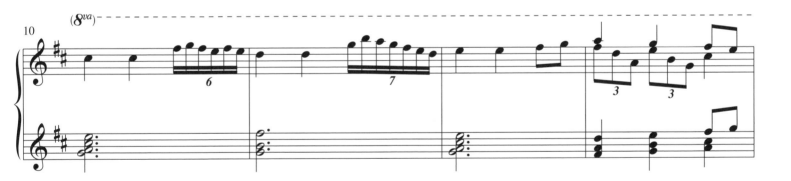

ANGELS WE HAVE HEARD ON HIGH

Arranged by
PHILIP KERN (ASCAP)

Tune: **GLORIA**
Traditional French Carol

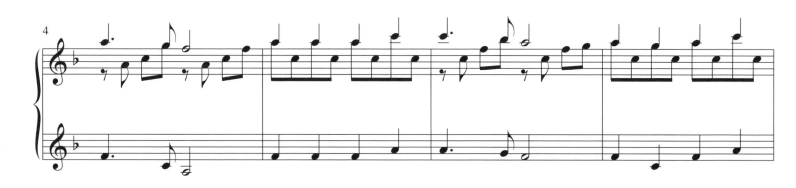

HE IS BORN, THE DIVINE CHRIST CHILD

Arranged by
PHILIP KERN (ASCAP)

Tune: **IL EST NÉ**
Traditional French Carol

WEXFORD CAROL

Arranged by
PHILIP KERN (ASCAP)

Traditional Irish Carol

GESÙ BAMBINO

Arranged by
PHILIP KERN (ASCAP)

Music by
PIÉTRO A. YON (1886-1943)

35027868

WE THREE KINGS

Arranged by
PHILIP KERN (ASCAP)

Tune: **KINGS OF ORIENT**
by JOHN HENRY HOPKINS, JR. (1820-1891)

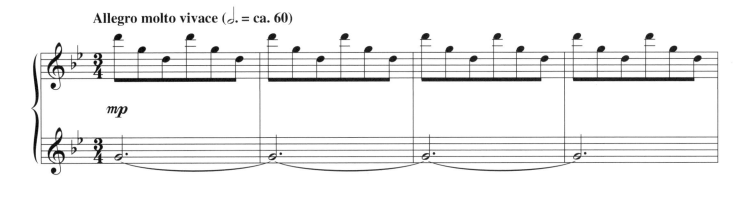

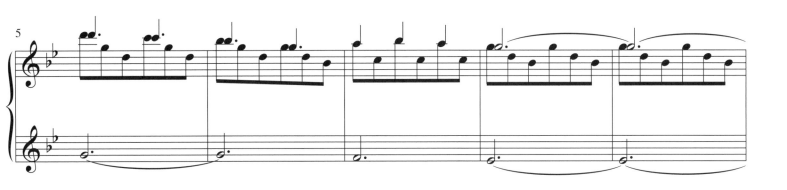

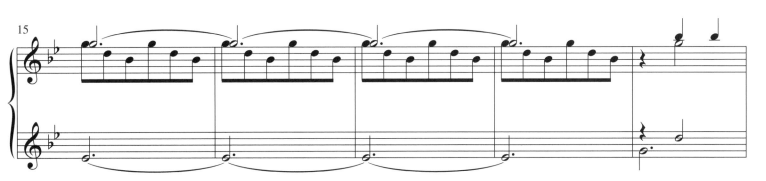

* S.P. = sostenuto pedal. This is the middle pedal. It is used to sustain the initial low notes and cleanly articulate the rest of the measures.

35027868

SILENT NIGHT, HOLY NIGHT

Arranged by
PHILIP KERN (ASCAP)

Tune: **STILLE NACHT**
by FRANZ GRÜBER (1787-1863)

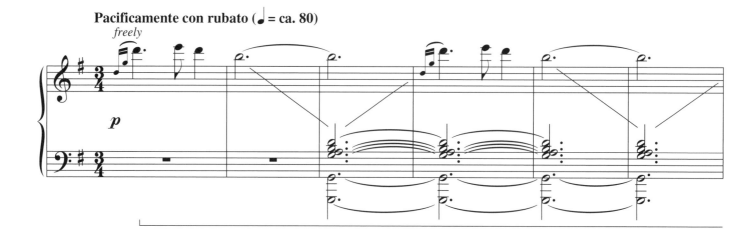

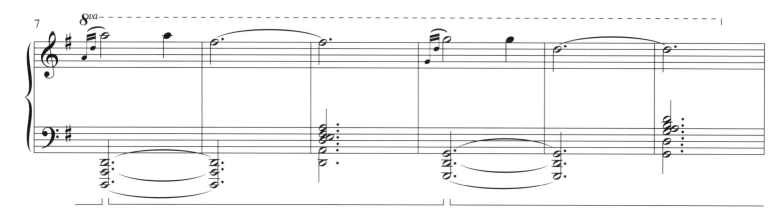